Birthing Your Destiny

Dr. Shirley K. Clark

PURPOSE & DESTINY SERIES, VOL. 2

Dr. Shirley K. Clark

Learn How to Release the
Greatness of God that is Within
You to Obtain Your Destiny

Birthing YOUR DESTINY

Dr. Shirley K. Clark

Unless otherwise noted, scriptural quotations are taken from the King James Version of the Bible.

Birthing Your Destiny
Copyright © 2013 Revised Edition
Shirley Clark International Ministries
www.drshirleyclark.org
Library of Congress — Cataloged in Publication Data

Printed in the United States

Ebook: 978-1-312-83567-2
Paperback: 978-1-3128-3564-1
Hardback: 978-1-312-83566-5

Published by Jabez Books
(A Division of Clark's Consultant Group)
www.clarksconsultantgroup.com
972424-2074 (ofc)

All Rights Reserved. No part of this book may be reproduced or transmitted in any form or by any means, electronically or mechanically, including photocopying recording, or by any other information storage and retrieval system, without permission in writing from the publisher.

1. Destiny | 2. Personal Success | 3. Vision

Dedication

This book is dedicated to all my spiritual Fathers and Mothers that birthed me and poured into my life throughout my walk with the Lord.

- The Late Bishop Mack Timberlake, Jr. & Pastor Brenda Timberlake, Former Pastors

- Pastor Lawrence Turner, Spiritual Father

- Pastor Anne Logan, Intercessory Prayer Instructor

- Pastor Mark Chironna, Former Pastor

- Bishop T. D. & Serita Jakes, Current Pastors
- The Late Pastor Rupert Dudley, Evangelistic Trainer

- The Late "Mama" Tina Blakely, Crusade Trainer

- The Late Pastor Thomas Branch, Biblical Trainer

I am who I am because of all of these leaders. I am so very grateful to all of them!

Thank You

- Thurman Clark, Jr. , My husband

- Family & Friends who supported me throughout this past year

- Patricia Scott, Copy Editor

- Cathy Johnson, Copy Editor

Dr. Shirley K. Clark

Other Books By
Dr. Shirley K. Clark

Pray & Grow Richer
Discovering Your Destiny
Birthing Your Destiny
Intercessors' Insights
Spiritual Warfare Teaching Manual and Workbook
The Ministry of Intercession
Prepare For War
Personal Spiritual Warfare
Pray, Push & Prevail
Strategic Warfare
The Midnight Cry
Empowering Your City
The Power of the "IF" Prayer Manual
52 Laws of Prayer

Dr. Shirley K. Clark

Table of Contents

Chapter 1
Principles of Birthing   13

Chapter 2
Stages of Birthing   39

Chapter 3
Elijah's Pattern   133

Dr. Shirley K. Clark

Chapter 1
Principles of Birthing

Dr. Shirley K. Clark

Principle One: Birthing is a Kingdom Principle

When we talk about birthing a destiny, the first thing we need to know is that birthing is a kingdom principle. It is a principle that originated from God. God always does things based on principle. When God wanted to make a change in the universe, the first thing He did was get in a birthing position. Genesis 1:2 says, *"And the earth was without form, and void; and darkness was upon the face of the deep. AND THE SPIRIT OF GOD MOVED UPON THE FACE OF THE WATERS."*

"Spirit of God moved upon" – means to hover or brood like a bird over its young, to warm them, and develop their vital powers. Deuteronomy 32:11, says, **"As a eagle stirreth up her nest, fluttereth over her young, spreadeth abroad her wings, taketh them, beareth them on her wing."**

The word, "brooding" in the commentary denotes a work in the actual process of accomplishment. It is a force that causes a reorganization of things. So looking at all of this, then if change is to be initiated, then being in the birthing position is the desired posture.

Principle Two: We Are All Birthed Out of Something

In Dr. Walter Fletcher's book, **Recovering the Soul**, it says, "To a certain degree we are all shaped by the cultural norms and values in which we are born. This may be a good thing, or it may be a hard shell we have to break out of in order to find our own identity and purpose."[1] This is so true. Because whether you were reared in an African-American family or an Asian-American family; whether you were from a Catholic or Pentecostal background or whether you were surrounded by negative or positive influences growing up, you were birthed out of something.

And whatever that something was or is, has defined your present and might possibly shape your future. The reason I said might possibly shape your future is because your future is yet to be defined. Remember, you can't change your past, but you can change your future. But whatever choices you make today, will define your future. The key here,

> *Because someone had a horrible past, does not negate them from having a successful future.*

however, your past does not have to equate to your future.

Some of the things many in the body of Christ have encountered in their past have been horrendous. However, because someone had a horrible past, does not negate them from having a successful future. We all have to reconcile with our past and/or come to peace with it if we are going to obtain our God ordained destiny. So your past is never an indication of your future. I believe the best way perhaps; to state this is, how you process your past will determine your future.

Mentoring is another form of being birthed out of or from something. It is a father-son, mother-daughter, and teacher-student relationship. How a mentor trains a person can affect the actions or responses of that person. Also, your identity is formed based on what you have been birthed out of as well.

Principle Three: Every Person, Place or Thing has a Destiny

God created all things, and all things were created for and with a purpose. *"For by him were all things created, that are in heaven, and that are in earth, visible and invisible, whether*

by thrones, or dominions, or principalities or powers; all things were created by him, and for him."

God is a God of purpose. Because of this everything that exists has a defined destination. You have a fixed purpose and destiny. In Rick Warren's book, **The Purpose Driven Life**, it says, "The purpose of your life is far greater than your own personal fulfillment."[2] God has a predetermined destiny for you.

> **"And hath made of one blood all nations of men for to dwell on all the face of the earth, and hath determined the times before appointed, and**

the bounds of their habitation."

Acts 17:26

"Predetermined" in Ephesians 1:3-6 means to set bounds before; predetermine limits. No matter how well you have etched out your future through career planning, if it is not God's plan and purpose for your life; then you are technically out of the will of God.

God has a prophetic destiny for your life and He wants to release it through you. But it can only be released through obedience and prayer on your part. You must seek Him to acquire His destiny for your life.

Is Your Destiny a Dream or a Fantasy?

Occasionally, I run into people who have very lofty dreams and visions. And because of my innate proclivity to encourage people to release the gifts of God out of their lives, automatically, I will initially applaud them for their aspirations and their ability to dream. But in several of these instances as time passed and I am able to assess these individuals' lifestyle and emotional and financial stamina, I realize many of these lofty ideas are

> *Authentic dreams and visions are what God is interested in birthing out in our lives.*

not only self-induced dreams, but it is a fantasy for *these* individuals.

Authentic dreams and visions are what God is interested in birthing out in our lives. If a dream or vision is not tied into our destiny; then perhaps, we are functioning out of a "fantasy mentality." Webster' defines dream as a sequence of sensations, images, and thoughts, passing through a person's mind. On the other hand, Webster defines fantasy as imagination and fancy: wild, a bizarre mental image, illusions, and an odd notion.[3]

Too many of God's people are laboring from a bizarre mental image or illusion. When the purpose of God is not clearly defined in our lives; then a lot of energy is wasted on developing and nurturing projects that are futile.

Dreams and visions are never realized from a fantasy mentality. God-given dreams and visions are images that have the power within them to be fulfilled. These are the dreams and visions that release change(s) in our lives and draw us toward our ultimate destiny.

Finding You

I watched a movie a few years ago and it was called ***"Finding Forrester."*** It was quite an intriguing movie from the beginning to the end. When I read the title, immediately, I thought;

> *We all have a core purpose for being in this world and if you are functioning outside of your authentic you; then your purpose will not be fulfilled.*

perhaps, this movie was going to be about a heroic adventure of a man named Forrester and how he was lost or got trapped in a cave or something of the such. But to my amazement it had nothing to do with a person being trapped in a cave or on a mountain. It was a story about a man named Forrester who was trapped internally. And because of his internal captivity, he lived a secluded life.

While he wanted to be free, his life's script that he wrote for himself would not allow him to do so.

The *fullness* of all that God has for you can only be realized when our internal voice is in harmony with God's voice. When this oneness is accomplished, you will then experience the authentic you. Your authentic self; is not defined by your job, education, income or role, but by who God ordained you to be. We all have a core purpose for being in this world and if you are functioning outside of your authentic you; then *your* purpose will not be fulfilled.

What we say in public is not what our lives will be shaped by. But it is what we say in private to ourselves that creates our world. Having internal dialogue is healthy. We need to constantly assess where we are internally and externally. But for the most part, for a significant amount of people in society, their internal dialogue is often distorted. If your internal dialogue is distorted long enough, then your world view

> *The thing that is so damaging to someone who is functioning out of a "fictional you" is that all of their sense of right and wrong, values, ideas and concepts will become warped.*

about yourself will be misconstrued. And if you continue to function out of this mindset, then having a faulty perception will become the norm for you.

We must see ourselves as God sees us. We are the apple of God's eye. We are His beloved. He wants us to prosper. He wants us whole. And He wants us to reach our full potential in Him.

The thing that is so damaging to someone who is functioning out of a "fictional you" is that all of their sense of right and wrong, values, ideas and concepts will become warped. So when God wants to bless them, they perhaps, will see it as something else. What do you say about yourself when no one is around? Whatever you say is the true you. You are with no one more than yourself. So if what you say about yourself does not line up with God's Word, you have to discard it IMMEDIATELY!

Sometimes we can be too hard on ourselves. When you make a mistake, repent and keep going in the right direction. Don't over process mistakes. If you do, you will always come up with some warped conclusion. I like what Dr. Phillip McGraw, Ph.D says, "Self-talk has immediate and concrete consequences. For every thought you have, you have an instant change in your physiological system." Your thought will either make you feel like a success or failure.

Self-criticism can also have a cancerous affect on our lives, especially if we are looking through the wrong lenses. In Dr. McGraw's book, **Self Matters**, he tells a story about an experiment that was given to some students. The experiment was that the students had to wear some special eyeglasses that inverted images. The lenses turned everything upside down. He said for the first few days the students were

Our perception will be warped and what we allow to play in our heads will eventually be our destiny.

bumping into everything. They were bumping into desks, walking into walls and constantly falling. It was a chaotic situation.

But after several other days passed, they began to adapt to their fictional upside down world. He said their brains became accustomed to the distortion. They were no longer questioning their environment. This experiment went on for a month and the student reported that the eyeglasses were no longer a problem. Their normal activities were almost the same.

The purpose of this experiment was to show how people quickly adapt to distorted information and perception. If we lend our ears to the sayings of the devil, then we will function out of a "fictional world" as well.

Our perception will be warped and what we allow to play in our heads will eventually be our destiny. Adam and Eve in the book of Genesis is an excellent example of this. They allowed the devil to "mess with their heads" by projecting erroneous thoughts at them. And because their perception was tampered with, their destiny was largely affected by this. Too many of us are playing the wrong tape inside of our heads. We have to guard our minds and be careful what tape we allow it to entertain. Here are some attributes about tapes that Dr. McGraw says:

<u>A tape looks backward, to your past</u> – Too many of us are looking backward when God is trying to take us forward. Apostle Paul says, "I press toward the mark for the prize of the high calling of God in Christ Jesus." (Philippians 3:14)

<u>A tape expresses itself as a judgment about who you are in the present</u> – Your past test score is never your final exam. "There is therefore *now* no condemnation to them which are in Christ Jesus, who walk not after the flesh, but after the Spirit." (Romans 8:1)

<u>A tape predicts the outcome you will have in the future</u> – God holds our future in His hand and a tape is a duplicate copy not an original. "I will praise thee; for I am fearfully and wonderfully made: marvellous are thy works..." (Psalm 139:14)[4]

Lens and Filters

In a book I read, it said that we all see "our" world through lens and filters. And it is these lens and filters that affects our perception of things or the world. They will either give us an

> *Every human being's worldview is deeply affected and driven by the "lenses" they have on.*

accurate view of the world or a distorted view of the world around us.

Lenses deal with how we see and think through things on the subconscious level and filters deal with how we feel our way through things on a heart level. It also said, "Lenses color how we see or think through things. This means that every human being's worldview is deeply affected and driven by the "lenses" they have on. We all have lenses, but the critical issue is whether our lenses have been compromised or contaminated by the things we have been through that are contrary to the Word of God."

When he talked about filters, he shared how every human being's worldview is deeply affected and driven by the filters they have over their heart.

When assessing who we are, we must look into the perfect law of liberty (the Bible) to determine who we really are. ***"But whoso looketh into the perfect law of liberty, and continueth therein, he being not a forgetful hearer, but a doer of the work, this man shall be blessed in his***

deed" (James 1:25). Always remember, God's investment in you is eternal.

Chapter 2
Stages of Birthing

There are three primary stages of birthing your dreams and destiny:

1. **Preparation**
2. **Position, and**
3. **Perseverance**

While some might be inclined to skip a stage - don't! If your dreams and visions are to come to pass in their full manifestation, then going through each stage is a necessity. You must be prepared, positioned and continue to persevere if you want the destiny of God to be worked out in your life.

> *It is only when you see your present circumstances through the lens of purpose will you have the strength to endure the preparation stage.*

STAGE ONE: Preparation

1. You have to prepare for greatness.

Most people in the body of Christ want to do great things for God, but they don't want to do the thing that fosters great-ness and that is to prepare.

The preparation stage is the most dreaded stage. Yet, it is one of the most pivotal components in your destiny being fulfilled in its entirety. Preparation is what you do in anticipation of a season that does not yet exist.[46]

"Prepare" means to make ready, suitable, to make receptive, to equip or furnish, to put together, construct, compound, to frame, to fortify, to brace or to strengthen.[47] The word "prepare" is listed in almost every book in the Old Testament.

Before Esther was crowned queen in the book of Esther in the Bible, she had to be prepared for greatness. For one year she had to endure a preparation stage. For the first six months she was purged with a bitter resin and the last six months she was anointed with precious ointments and fragrances.

I can imagine Esther in the first six months being really challenged by the purification process. But I believe as she was going through this process, God gave her a glimpse of her future. It is only when you see your present circumstances through the lens of purpose will you have the strength to endure the preparation stage. I read once that the definition of endurance is to be left standing when all others have collapsed. Endurance is fortified in the preparation stage.

Having An Open Womb: Conception can only take place in an open womb. When the virgin Mary was visited by an angel of God who told her that she was going to conceive a son and that He would save His people from sin, she replied, ***"...be it unto me according to thy word" Luke 1:32-34.***

When Mary said this, this became a role model for generations of chosen vessels according to David Yeazell in his book, <u>The baby: Life Cycle of a Kingdom Vision."</u> He further says:

> ***"Be it unto me"*** *is the response of one not impressed by the fact that they have never been pregnant*

or birthed before. It is, in essence, the only reply suitable to the Divine Lover, who saw a purity and willingness of heart in Mary, as He does in us when He visits us with a word, or promise of purpose and destiny.

In the hour of our visitation, we may wonder at the words of the message, and question the status of our ability to conceive; but it is when the Beloved Himself validates the call to conception with the promise of His overshadowing our human limitations that our response should parallel Mary's willingness. Having an open spiritual womb means the interior place in our being will become home for and nurture something that will grow bigger than, and beyond our greatest expectations and human limitations.

As a type of surrogate parent, we get the privilege of being a vessel to carry another's vision, and the other just happens to be the Beloved. An open spiritual womb means that the tender, nutritiously lined place that is the fountainhead of personal prayer, spiritual ministry and kingdom fruit will welcome one that will attach itself in dependence and over the months draw from its lifeline of intercession and spiritual power as it develops and grows.

And from that inner tender place, the protected vision will be able to form from the smallest of frames until the moment when the thing has grown so huge that it is pressed against the nutritious walls until they are able to stretch no more; and feeling the constraints of its surroundings, and waiting to transition outside to its destiny, it begins to kick the boundaries of the womb of the willing vessel.

2. Preparation is synonymous with victory.

Proverbs 16:1 says, "The preparation of the heart in man, and the answer of the tongue, is from the Lord." Preparation is the foundation for success in life.

> *If you want the purpose and destiny of God to be worked out in your life, then you need to prepare for greatness.*

When you are properly prepared, this positions you for victory. Some people don't want to prepare for anything. It is just like being in school.

If you prepared for the test or exam, then the odds were in your favor to make a good grade. If you did not prepare, most likely, you did not do as well. So if you wanted to do well on a test, then you had to prepare. If you want the purpose and destiny of God to be worked out in your life, then you need to prepare for greatness. Preparation equals victory.

3. Preparation is always part of God's strategic plan.

Proverbs 20:18, "Every purpose is established by counsel: and with good advice make war." Counsel helps establish purpose. Corporate

America has instituted this formula all so well. When corporations are planning to make a change within their organization that might largely affect their image to consumers; they first have roundtable dialogue to discuss the possible reactions they might encounter from the change for consumers. It is out of these meetings that a strategic marketing plan is compiled.

In the body of Christ we must do the same. We must be strategic. On an individual basis, strategic planning or counsel can be your best friend. **Luke 14:31 says, "Or what king, going to make war against another king, sitteth not down first, and consulteth whether he be able**

with ten thousand to meet him that cometh against him with twenty thousand?"

Annually, I host International Prayer Clinics in Dallas, TX. In 2003, God instructed me to begin to bring in national speakers. Since I had never done this before, I immediately began to seek counsel from various leaders and pastors what to expect and how to host these individuals. I wanted to know what were the pitfalls as well as the mindsets of national speakers. There were three people I sought counsel from before embarking upon this new phase: Pastor Brenda Timberlake, Senior Pastor of Christian Faith Center; Lady Beverly Robinson, Executive

Administrative Assistant for Bishop T. D. Jakes, and Apostle Phyllis Terry, Co-Pastor of God's Way Love Center.

The information I received from each of these individuals was invaluable, and because I sought counsel, I had a very successful conference. Everything ran like clockwork. My speakers were attended to properly. In fact, both of the two speakers that we invited have embraced the ministry and me, and inadvertently, I gained new friends. You see, you must be organized and strategic when executing the plan of God for your life.

4. Preparation is never lost time

My former pastor, Bishop Mack Timberlake, Jr. taught me that preparation is never lost time. You can never lose by preparing yourself. I would rather be overly prepared than under prepared. You can only gain when you are prepared. Being prepared will cause you to be at ease or more relaxed when having to deal with the vicissitudes and adversities of life. Preparing properly will generate a

> *Preparing properly will generate a cycle of success in your life.*

cycle of success in your life. If you would be honest, the time you waste from not being prepared is far greater than the time you consume when you are prepared.

When God prepares you, it is done with your future in mind. Often this is the last conclusion that is discovered when trying to process a current negative situation. While God is concerned about your present state, His ultimate goal is your destiny. He wants you to reach your full potential. Sometimes He prepares you for things that you will walk into twenty to thirty years later.

5. Preparation brings favor

It is in the preparation stage also that you acquire favor for your destiny. Esther received favor for her destiny while she was in the preparation stage. ***"...And the king loved Esther above all the women, and she obtained grace and favor in his sight more than all the virgins" (Esther 2:17).*** Esther not only received favor from the king, but her attendants also favored her – ***"...And Esther obtained favor in the sight of all them that looked upon her" (Esther 2:15).*** I have learned over the years that favor is always attached to purpose. You cannot have one without the other.

Psalm 5:22 says, "For thou, Lord, wilt bless the righteous; with favour wilt thou compass him as with a shield."

6. Provision is released in the preparation stage

The preparation stage is also the stage where provision is made available for your destiny. This is an essential part of the preparation stage because of the type of warfare that lies ahead for you. Because

> *Because favor is attached to purpose, it will cause people to favor you.*

favor is attached to purpose, it will cause people to favor you. Often when this happens, God will use people to provide for your needs. While you might be encountering warfare on one hand, God simultaneously on the other hand raises up people to comfort you during your warfare. He has done this repeatedly in my life.

7. The preparation stage is the weeding stage

The preparation stage is important also because God uses this stage as a weeding process. This is the stage where God weeds out of your life negative thoughts and unhealthy relationships that are detrimental to your destiny. If this process of elimination is not done, your destiny will be affected largely by these negative factors. Sometimes you are required to give up what you think are good things, but keep in mind God knows what is best for you.

> *Sometimes you are required to give up what you think are good things, but keep in mind God knows what is best for you.*

As my personal ministry began to grow, I heard God tell me it was time to release a dear friend of mine. He said where you are going she will frustrate your purpose. Not that she would intentionally do this, but her natural personality and proclivity will become a strain for me. I had known her for over twenty years and God was now telling me to release her. Not out of my life per se', but I could not spend as much time with her like I had in the past.

When God first spoke this to me, I felt a ripping in my flesh. Sometimes you are so close to people that it is extremely hard to release them. I was so accustomed to picking up the telephone to call and talk to her weekly or biweekly that one day out of habit I picked up the telephone to call her. Immediately, the Spirit of God resounded in my spirit and said, "Put the phone down." I instantly obeyed. It was hard to cut the umbilical cord that tied us together, but three years later, I fully understood why God asked me to release this individual. You must obey God no matter how hard it seems.

The condition of the mother always affects the health of the baby. When the mother is healthy, then there is a greater chance that the baby will be healthy. If the mother is sick, then most likely the baby will be affected by this abnormality. Whatever is going on in your life whether it is healthy or unhealthy, it will affect the outcome of your destiny.

When God plants a seed in your heart (spirit), you have to protect and preserve the seed that is growing inside of you. Some in the body of Christ are called to birth nations. Some are called to affect their generation. Whatever He is calling you into; you must protect the seed at all cost.

> *When God plants a seed in your heart (spirit), you have to protect and preserve the seed that is growing inside of you.*

In the book of Genesis when Rebekah, Isaac's wife, was pregnant with twins, God spoke to her and told her that she had two nations growing inside of her.

> *"And Isaac intreated the Lord for his wife, because she was barren: and the Lord was intreated of him, and Rebekah his wife conceived...And the Lord said unto her, **two nations** are in thy womb."*
> Genesis 25:21, 23

It is amazing how God sees things. We see a fetus, while God sees nations. The birth of John the Baptist is another example of someone being pregnant with greatness.

*"But the angel said unto him, Fear not, Zachariah; for thy prayer is heard, and thy wife Elisabeth shall bear thee a son, and thou shalt call his name John...**For he shall be great in the sight of the Lord**...he shall be filled with the Holy Ghost, **even from his mother's womb**..."*
Luke 1:13, 15

Both of these people were pregnant with greatness. Today, I want to ask you, "What's in your belly?"

Every preparation stage is different. God knows what it will take to prepare you for your destiny. It might take you ten years to reach your destiny, but it might take someone else five years. Everyone has a different preparation stage. This is why you should never compare yourself with others. God has a precise time for your destiny to come to pass.

8. Why do you need to be prepared?

You need to prepare because there is a pending war that is inevitably attached to your destiny. Your destiny will determine your warfare! I heard my pastor, Bishop T. D. Jakes say it this way, "The level of your trouble is the level of your destiny."

You must have a militant mindset when pursuing His will for your life; especially when you do not see any fruit being manifested in the natural.

Joel 3:9 says, "...**Prepare war**, wake up the mighty men, let all the men of war draw near, let them come up: beat your plowshares into swords, and your pruninghooks into spears: let the weak say, I am strong."

It was because of Joseph's destiny that he endured such persecution and betrayal from his family in Genesis 37. When Joseph shared his destiny with his family, they forsook him and sold him to the Ishmaelites. This was a treacherous act for loved ones to do to another loved one. However, it was Joseph's destiny that brought about this warfare.

This is why the Lord wants to prepare you for war, so that you might obtain your future. You must have a militant mindset when pursuing His will for your life; especially when you do not see any fruit being manifested in the natural.

STAGE TWO: Position

1. The sooner you get in the birthing position, the sooner your dreams and visions will come to pass.

God impregnates every generation with a new move of God

Isaiah 66:8 says, **"...For as soon as Zion travailed, she brought forth her children."** The sooner you get in the birthing position; the sooner life will be birthed through you. You must be properly positioned if you want the destiny of God to be birthed in your life. Too many Christians are improperly or inappropriately positioned. This is a pervasive problem in the body of Christ. If you want God to birth greatness through you, then there must be a season of travail.

God impregnates every generation with a new move of God. Therefore, being in the birthing position gives opportunities for the will of God to be released. You see; the enemy of your future is always resistant to change. God is notorious for introducing the new in the midst of the old. God will upset the old order that a new government might be established.

The birth of Christ is an accurate example of God releasing a new order in the midst of the old. It was a governmental and headship change. Whenever there is a governmental and headship change, the existing edicts and legislative protocols will no doubt have to be altered as well. For the most part this will not be a smooth transition. The

> *When people's minds are cloaked and bound by tradition, then releasing the newness of God into the earth becomes a tug-of-war.*

old will always fight for its credibility to maintain its existence.

When King Herod, in the book of Matthew, Chapter Two, heard that a new king (government) was scheduled to arise, he immediately became threatened and tried to discredit and destroy the new move of God. But his efforts were to no avail. When God initiates change in a situation, no matter what kind of scheme or tactic the devil conjures up, God's will, will be done.

Releasing the newness of God into the earth has always been a battle throughout church history. Much of the warfare that the church is encountering today is on a totally different level than twenty or thirty years ago. Because of this, new revelation must be released in the earth so that we can outwit and pull down these strongholds. When people's minds are cloaked and bound by tradition, then releasing the newness of God into the earth becomes a tug-of-war. However, releasing the newness of God is essential for the church, if the church is to be effective in the now.

The church can no longer expect the "Goliaths" of this era to be brought down with a slingshot and a rock. The "Goliaths" of this time are more sophisticated and clever. Their tactics are seductive and their maneuvers are more deadly. This is why, today, the church must seek

God for new tactics and strategies to outwit the enemy. Old and outdated strategies are no longer effective in this present warfare. So if the church continues to use such nomadic and primitive tactics, then instead of it being a place of refuge it will become a place of ruin. The church needs new wineskin to accommodate the present move of God.

New wineskin, New revelation
New wineskin, New move of God

Every dream, destiny or vision has to be birthed in the spirit first before it is manifested in the natural. What Simeon saw in the spirit first, Mary brought forth in the natural (Luke 2:25-35). **II Corinthians 4:18 says it this way, "While we look not at the things which are seen, but at the things which are not seen: for the things which are seen are temporal; but the things which are not seen are eternal."**

> *In order for the blessings to be released in the earth, there must be a season of travail; someone must birth them into existence.*

It is the eternal things of God that you should be panting after. God is looking for a people He can impregnate with His vision. God is looking for a people who have the spirit of the midwife upon their lives. God is looking for a people whom He can birth something through -- people who are going to take their position on their birthing stool.

Ephesians 1:3 says "Blessed be the God and Father of our Lord Jesus Christ, who hath blessed us with all spiritual blessings in heavenly places in Christ." I know many get excited about this scripture, but the thing that is often overlooked is that it says that the blessings are in *heavenly places*. Meaning, they are not accessible yet on earth. In order for the blessings to be released in the earth, there must be a season of travail; someone must birth them into existence. The church is the bride of Christ and God wants her to join Him in His bedchamber.

"...As soon as Zion travail." In the Greek the word "travail" means to labor, painful effort; it stresses the toil involved in work; birth pang, great tribulation; to bear a child, to writhe; hardship; exertion; to suffer; to agonize.[8] There is nothing that is worth achieving that comes easily. And there is nothing about the word, "travail" that sounds good. In the Bible it is used 45 times and out of the 45 times 34 times it was used in reference to birthing.

The question you need to ask yourself today is how bad do you want your blessing? How bad do you want the destiny and purpose of God to be fulfilled in your life? How bad do you want God's dreams and vision to come to pass in your life? If you want it bad enough, then you won't mind the temporary discomfort for a season – "...For as soon as Zion travailed, *she brought forth...*"

2. Inside every believer there are living waters waiting to be released.

John 7:38 says, "He that believeth on me, as the scripture hath said, out of his belly shall flow rivers of living waters."

God has ordained living waters to flow out of your belly. God wants you to birth life and not death. The word, "belly" (Koilia) in the Greek means innermost part of a womb.[9] A womb is a birthing canal. A womb is a developmental station. Out of your belly, God has prescribed streams of glory to come forth. And out of this glory new dimensions of the kingdom will develop.

What will these new dimensions do? They will destroy the spirit of Saul -- the jealousy spirit (it is the spirit that insecure fathers/pastors are birthed out of; which tries to destroy their own sons and daughters' destiny); the spirit of Absalom -- the spirit that undermines leadership in the body of Christ; the spirit of Jezebel -- the spirit that tries to thwart prophetic insight and revelation in the church (control spirit); and the spirit of Laban – the spirit of deception.

> *The Spirit of God will give substance to that you are positioned properly to bring forth.*

God is trying to raise up apostolic houses (churches) all throughout the nations. God is transitioning the church from a church mentality to a kingdom mentality. But to transition the church from a church mentality to a kingdom mentality will require that a new order be established. The government of God can only be established when you allow room within your spirit for the newness of God to be birthed.

However, how you react or function in your individual destiny will affect the overall effectiveness of the kingdom of God. The body of Christ is fitly jointed together. The sum of the force of the kingdom of God is determined by each intricate part. The old adage is true, "We are as strong as our weakest point."

Remember, you are the conduit and the Holy Spirit is the birthing agent. The Spirit of God will give substance to that you are positioned properly to bring forth. **"...for we know not what we should**

pray for as we ought: but the Spirit itself maketh intercession for us with groanings which cannot be uttered" *(Romans 8:26).*

The Spirit of God is ever-present to birth the will of the Father into existence. Jesus declared when He walked upon this earth that He was here to do the will of the Father. If Jesus understood how important it was for the will of God to be accomplished, then how much more should you desire that His will be done in you and through you? Birthing the will and purpose of God for your life is always a courtship between the Holy Spirit and you.

3. The believer's birthing chamber is the prayer closet

If you want to find out what God has for you to do, then you have to spend some time with Him. It is in your time spent alone with the Father that He will reveal His heart to you. Your courtship with the Father cannot be a "one night stand" or a "weekend hotel visit." Rather, it must be a relationship that is developed through a constant abiding in His presence. The Psalmist says in Chapter 91, **"He that dwelleth in the secret place of the most High**

You must be in God's face, so He can show you His glory and His heart.

shall abide under the shadow of the Almighty."

"Dwelleth" means to sit; abiding where God abides.[50] The idea is that of having one's home or residence in the most holy place in the tabernacle.

So many people struggle and are plagued mentally about not knowing the will of God for their lives. But it is in the birthing chamber (your prayer closet) that the plan and purpose of God for your life will be revealed. You must be in God's face, so He can show you His glory and His heart. What you behold is what you become!

When Jacob was struggling within himself about the outcome of his future, it was only when He saw God face to face that his destiny was disclosed – ***"And Jacob called the name of the place Peniel: for I have seen God face to face, and my life is preserved*** (Genesis 32:30).

After Jacob wrestled with an angel all night, God spoke into his life and his name was changed from Jacob to Israel. In one moment his entire destiny was revealed to him. God, in essence, told Jacob that he was no longer going to operate out of his past mindset, but he was going to be a man of God whose life would mirror victory and success from that day forward. His mindset shifted and the plan and purpose of God for his life was unfolded overnight. Jacob's previous nature was one of a trickster and deceiver, but his new identity reflected the prevailing nature of God.

The birthing chamber is not only a place of rest and solitude, but it is a haven for purpose to be realized.

STAGE THREE: Perseverance

1. God's desire is that your destiny be manifested in its fullness.

Perseverance is the trait that helps facilitate your destiny reaching its full potential. It is a key ingredient in the process. Therefore, it is essential that you remain on your "birthing stool" until change comes. Great things have always happened to those who persevere. Winners are never quitters. Winners have always been those willing to try one more time.

> *When your dreams and visions are unfolded, a new level of glory will be released at each dimension.*

In the pursuit of purpose, we must persevere at all cost. Regardless of opposition, we must persevere. Perseverance will always outlast persecution. If we want something bad enough; then we must persevere. The proof of desire is pursuit. So what God is after in this stage is mature sons and daughters (dreams/visions) being manifested. There is a manifest glory that God wants to release into your life, but it can only be released out of maturity. The fulfillment of your dreams will give glory to God. *"For I reckon that the sufferings of this present time are not worthy to be compared with the glory which shall be revealed in us" (Romans 8:18).* I just had a friend who shared with me that God spoke to her and said, "The body of Christ has definitely had its share of the fellowship of its suffering, but He is about to let them experience the power of His resurrection." At each level of maturity in your life, there is a level of glory associated with it.

> *It is said some people succeed because they are destined, but most people succeed because they are determined.*

This is a parallel truth with your dreams and visions. When your dreams and visions are unfolded, a new level of glory will be released at each dimension. The normal process or cycle is to go from glory to glory. Every level of glory will release a new revelation or insight into your destiny.

And the levels of glories you have *not* reached will serve as an invisible cord (placed in your life by God) to keep you from being stuck in your present state. Its existence is to pull and cradle you into your God-given destiny.

2. Some believers are getting off their birthing stools too early

If change is to occur in your situation and life, then you must persevere and stay on your "birthing stool." You must pray and pray until you see the full manifestation of your prayers. What we are willing to invest in reveals what we *really* want. It is said some people succeed because they are destined, but most people succeed because they are determined. Your desire to see the will of God manifested in your life will cause you to go the extra mile and push a little harder. No burning desire, then there will be no perseverance.

You must have passion for your purpose. Passion is an intense or strong desire. Fulfilling your passion in life is what separates the haves and the have-nots. Passion fuels our purpose on earth. This is why we must stay focused and never get off of our birthing stool.

But in case you wander down the road of disbelief, and you get off of your "birthing stool" too soon, two things could happen:

A. Your dreams and visions may be deformed or you might have a premature fetus.

Isaiah 26:17-18 say, "Like a woman with child, that draweth near the time of her delivery...We have been with child, we have been in pain, we have as it were brought forth wind; we have not wrought any deliverance in the earth..."

Isaiah 37:3 says it this way, "...This day is a day of trouble, and of rebuke, and of blasphemy: for the children are come to the birth, and there is not strength to bring forth."

Perhaps, the reason there is no deliverance being wrought in your life or through your ministry is because you did not stay on your birthing stool long enough. The reason you are feeling so despondent is because you did not persevere until you saw change.

> *Ishmael was the son that Abraham and Sarah created, but Isaac was the son that God ordained.*

Yes, I know there will be warfare, but many of the wars you will encounter can only be won on your knees. Perseverance in prayer will solidify two things in your life: faith and determination.

Many of the things that you will endure getting to your "Promised Land" will be challenging; this is why you must stay on your birthing stool to maintain your focus and fortitude.

I have found in the past, when people do not stay on their birthing stools long enough, they end up settling for second best. This is a trick of the enemy. The enemy wants you to settle for the Ishmaels in your life and not the Isaacs.

Ishmael was the son that Abraham and Sarah created,

but Isaac was the son that God ordained (Genesis 15-17). This is a lesson for all of us; don't get ahead of God. Abraham and Sarah got ahead of God and because of their misguided efforts; they created a situation that God could only rectify. Out of His mercy, He salvaged the situation.

Despite Ishmael's parents' misguided efforts, God blessed him. Anyway, why should Ishmael be punished for his parents' fault? In fairness to

> *When you are pregnant with destiny, you have to be careful that you do not allow situations, traumas and mishaps to destroy your destiny.*

Ishmael, God allowed some of the Abrahamic blessings to flow in his life. But this is the problem with the "Ishmaels" in life. Because the "Ishmaels" are blessed, sometimes they have the tendency to resemble the "Isaacs."

One thing you must always remember, Isaac was the promised child not Ishmael. Therefore, you need to seek out to bring forth the promised child (God ordained destiny) for your life rather than settling for second best.

Discernment will be needed to distinguish between the two. I am not saying this is an easy task to master because it takes an incredible amount of discernment to be able to make the distinction at times. However, it can be done.

The anointing and blessing that is often associated with the Ishmaels can be very attractive and tantalizing. But no matter how enticing the Ishmaels might look in your life, God's covenant generational blessings are upon the Isaacs only.

"And Abraham said unto God, O that Ishmael might live before thee!

And God said, Sarah thy wife shall bear thee a son indeed, and thou shalt call his name

Isaac: and I will establish my covenant with him for an everlasting covenant, and with his seed after him.

*And as for Ishmael, I have heard thee: behold, **I have blessed him, and will make him fruitful, and will multiply him exceedingly; twelve princes shall he beget, and I will make him a great nation.** But my covenant will I establish with Isaac."*

Genesis 17:18-21

God has an everlasting covenant weaved into your destiny. I would rather own the bank than be the governor over the estate. This is the difference.

B. Dreams and visions may be aborted

If you don't properly protect and monitor the seed that God has placed inside of you, then destruction could be the end. Ultimately, this is the enemy's desire – to destroy your vision. When you are pregnant with destiny, you have to be careful that you do not allow situations, traumas and mishaps to destroy your destiny.

Bad news and disappointments in life can destroy hope. Hope is the thing that keeps your dream alive. If hope is ever tampered with, it will open the door for doubt and unbelief to fester in your life. Once this occurs, the enemy dispatches demonic spirits to utterly destroy you.

Phinehas' wife, in the book of Samuel, allowed this to happen to her. She allowed a bad situation to destroy her destiny. She was right at the point of delivery, but because she was not watchful, she allowed bad news to abort her destiny.

When Phinehas' wife heard that the ark of God was taken from them and that her husband was killed in battle, she became so distraught that she opened the door for the enemy to use this opportunity to destroy the remainder of her destiny. While I would admit these were devastating occurrences, you must learn how to harness your emotions during bad situations so that you might have faith and hope for the future.

The key to your success in this area is staying in the birthing position. Also, you must be watchful. At certain times this is more critical than others. Being at the point of delivery is one of them. Never take for granted that just because you have been successful three-fourths of the way, the other one-fourth would be the same. In fact, expect turbulence. So fasten your seat belt because you will be heading for a bumpy ride.

Another aspect of aborting the plan and purpose of God for your life is when you are walking in your destiny and you allow the spirit of disobedience and pride to operate in your life. King Saul is a perfect example of this. Even though Saul had reached his destiny, but because of disobedience and pride, the kingdom was stripped prematurely from him. God had a plan for Saul's life. But because he did not stay in a place where God could continue to use him, he had to be removed. This was not God's original intent for Saul.

When God chose Saul the scriptures said he was a godly man, he was pure in heart, he had strong leadership skills and he was anointed for the job (I Samuel 9:2, 10:1).

But when Saul transitioned to the position of a king, he allowed all kind of negative spirits to operate in his life – rebellion, pride, jealousy, murder, disobedience, etc. The lack of conviction in his life to repent was also the thing that Saul was judged by largely. Saul no longer had a heart to follow God. All of these things caused Saul to lose the kingdom.

Listen to what the scripture had to say as the kingdom was being stripped from Saul:

"Then came the word of the Lord unto Samuel, saying, It repenteth me that I have set up Saul to be King: for he is turned back from following me, and hath not performed my commandments...When thou wast little in thine own sight, wast thou not made the head of the tribes of Israel, and the Lord anointed thee king over Israel?...

For rebellion is as the sin of witchcraft, an stubbornness is as iniquity and idolatry.

Because thou hast rejected the word of the Lord, he hath also rejected thee from being king."

I Samuel 15: 10-23

Saul's destiny was aborted because he got out of the Will of God for his life. When God promotes you, you have to fight constantly against the spirit of pride. If you don't monitor this area meticulously, it will slowly invade your personality. When you are promoted, you have to purpose in your heart even the more to stay humble. I Peter 5:5 tells us that we should be clothed with the spirit of humility. God looks for humble people to release and use for kingdom building. God can do so much more through you if you can only stay humble.

> *God can do so much more through you if you can only stay humble.*

Look at all God did through Moses: He used him to bring

down an entire kingdom of Egypt; ten miraculous plagues were released at his command; the Red Sea was parted and it was divided for a span of time long enough to allow millions of people to cross over; he struck a rock with a staff and water gushed out; he had a forty day face-to-face encounter with God. Yet, the Bible records that Moses was the most humble man there ever was (Number 12:3). No matter how much God uses you or elevates you, you must stay humble.

3. There is an appointed time for your destiny to come forth

When David was anointed to be king over Israel, he was yet a young lad and it was years later before he actually functioned in this capacity. However, at the time he was anointed, the mantle of a king fell upon his life, but the operational gift did not come until years later – ***"Then Samuel took the horn of oil, and anointed him in the midst of his brethren: and the Spirit of the Lord came upon David from that day forward"*** (I Samuel 16:13). He had to wait until God ordained the appointed time and season for this divine purpose to come forth.

**Ecclesiastes 3:1 says,
"To every thing there is
a season, and a time
to every purpose
under the heaven."**

Just because God has ordained or called you to be this or that, you still have to wait until God releases you to walk in it. Time is part of God's governmental protocol. Throughout the Bible phrases in regards to "time" were used repeatedly when individuals were told to expect certain things to happen in their lives.

"Is any thing too hard for the Lord? At the time

appointed I will return unto thee, according to the time of life, and Sarah shall have a son...For Sarah conceived, and bare Abraham a son in his old age, at the set time of which God had spoken to him."

Genesis 18:14, 21:2

"And the Lord appointed a set time, saying, To-morrow the Lord shall do this thing in the land. And the Lord did that thing on the morrow..."

Exodus 9:5

"And he said, about this season, according to the time of life, thou shalt embrace a son...And the woman conceived, and bare a son at that season that Elisha has said unto her, according to the time of life."

2 Kings 4:16-17

God has a set time and a season for destiny to be worked out in your life.

Personal Prophecy: The thing that is so wonderful about personal prophecy is that it really encourages and boosts your confidence and self-esteem. It often motivates you to do; when perhaps, you might have been squandering your time. However, the thing that God uses to stir you – personal prophecy – can also become a sword in your life. This has been a snare to many saints.

> *While you can assist your destiny in coming to pass through prayer and obedience, ultimately it is up to God when it will be realized.*

While you can assist your destiny in coming to pass through prayer and obedience, ultimately it is up to God when it will be realized. God has a perfect time for your destiny to come to pass. ***"And let us not be weary in well doing: for in due season we shall reap, if we faint not."*** Galatians 6:9

Wrong Motives: God is not mocked; therefore, He cannot be manipulated. Occasionally, you run into people who try to manipulate God through prayer. When they do this; however, it is not pleasing to God nor does it provoke their destiny to come to pass any quicker. In actuality, it hinders it. Being in God's perfect will for your life is the only avenue that will afford destiny to be worked out in your life. Your motive must be pure when desiring the things of God for your life.

Simon in the book of Acts, Chapter 8:18-19, had the wrong spirit and motive for desiring the power of God. "And when Simon saw that through laying on of the apostles' hands the Holy Ghost was given, he offered them money, saying, give me also this power, that on whomsoever I lay hands, he may receive the Holy Ghost."

Simon really wasn't concerned with the people being blessed or their needs being met, as it was he wanted "the power." He wanted to look like the apostles. He wanted to be the one that people looked up to. He wanted to be the "big shot" in other words. There are no short cuts to acquiring the things of God in your life. Your motive must be pure and you must understand timing; otherwise, you will become frustrated.

> *God is not punishing you when certain things do not come to pass in your life when you think it ought to.*

One of the hardest things to convince Christians to do is to stay consistent in the things of God when their dreams and visions have not realized in the time frame they expected. When things do not happen when they thought it should have, they stop being faithful.

They lay out of church. They stop tithing. Some lose hope. Others develop a critical spirit. And some might even backslide. The promises of God can only be obtained through faith and patience. Hebrews 6:12 confirms this, "That ye be not slothful, but followers of them who through faith and patience inherit the promises." **A promise has nothing to**

do with your yesterday, but everything to do with your future.

When I run into people who complain all the time about other people and ministries I know I am dealing with a person who has unfulfilled dreams and visions in their life. Out of their frustration and disappointment, they latch out at others who look successful; especially in the area they perceive they should be prospering. This is the wrong attitude, however, to form. This is a venomous trait that can only hinder and impede your vision and destiny from coming to pass even the more. You must fight against these thoughts and not allow them to fester and take root within your soul.

The Bible says God rains on the just and the unjust. God is not punishing you when certain things do not come to pass in your life when you think it ought to. God is a loving God and He knows what is best for you. He knows when you are ready to handle a certain blessing and when you are not. Habakkuk, Chapter 2:2 says that every vision has an appointed time – ***"For the vision is yet for an appointed time, but at the end it shall speak, and not lie: though it tarry, wait for it; because it will surely come, it will not tarry."***

David's kingship was predicated on his readiness to function as a king. There were many things David had to contend with (Saul trying to kill him, disgruntled warriors, the lack of leadership, driving out illegal squatters off their land, etc.) when he came into office. So God had to make sure David was equipped to handle the many responsibilities that would come with the job. Let's face it, sometimes you are not ready to handle the blessings that God has for your life.

I like the story of Zacharias and Elisabeth in the book of Luke, Chapter one verses 5-13. Their story depicts the caliber of people God wants His people to emulate. Even though their dreams and visions did not come to pass in their desired time, they stayed faithful to the things of God and in the house of the Lord.

When you read these passages of scripture you will ascertain that Zacharias and Elisabeth were righteous people. Zacharias was a priest and his wife, Elisabeth, was from the lineage of Aaron.

Being a priest was a very sacred position in the kingdom. It was the priest that was responsible for burnt offerings being sacrificed for the sins of the people. It was the priest that had to keep the altar of incense burning at all times in the house of the Lord. The priest had a very rigid, but sacred job.

Elisabeth coming from the lineage of Aaron also speaks volume. If you know anything about Aaron's pedigree, you would know that he was the one chosen to speak on behalf of Moses when Moses had to confront Pharaoh to release God's people. Aaron was also from the descendant of the Levites. Therefore, he was part of the priesthood family. So they both had a tremendous righteous heritage and legacy.

But everything was not right in their lives. The proverbial questions I am sure most people heard rings true here, "Why do bad things happen to good people?" For years they had desired a child, but they could not have one.

> *"And they were both righteous before God, walking in all the commandments and ordinances of the Lord blameless.*
>
> *And they had no child, because that Elisabeth was barren, and they both were now well stricken in years.*

And it came to pass, that while he executed the priest's office before God in the order of his course,

According to the custom of the priest's office, his lot was to burn incense when he went into the temple of the Lord."

Luke 1:6-9

According to these scriptures there were three things that they had to contend with:

    1. They had no child

    2. Elisabeth was barren

    3. They were stricken in age

But despite the fact that their hearts' desire had not come to pass, they were still faithful. We find Zacharias still performing his priestly duties in the house of Lord. He was still a seeker of God and he kept his prayer ritual. Elisabeth, likewise, maintained her righteous posture.

They did not stop going to church. They didn't resign from the committees/auxiliaries they were assigned to assist. They didn't give up on God. They continued to walk with Him. And right in the midst of them being faithful, God changed their situation instantly. The scriptures said *while* Zacharias was praying in the temple an angel appeared unto him and said your prayer has been answered. Your wife, Elisabeth, will bear a son and his name shall be called John.

You see; if you choose to have no children, this is your prerogative. But it is another thing to desire children and cannot have them. A lot of couples have chosen not to have children, but I have never known any woman who has chosen to be barren. Usually it is the opposite.

Because barrenness is such a pervasive problem in society many couples have paid countless dollars to doctors to assist them in having a child. Therefore, the scientific community has invented and discovered several alternative methods to assist in this process. Zachariah and Elisabeth had to struggle with this also.

Another thing they had to work through was that they were old and stricken in age. The odds are against you no matter what, when you are older and having a child. When your body reaches a certain age, physiological changes begin to take place that is not conducive to childbearing.

More abnormities can occur and you are susceptive to more complications. There are increased chances for a miscarriage. Everything pretty much becomes a threat to the baby's health and sometimes to the mother. No doubt Zachariah and Elisabeth had to overcome all of this mental anguish. They had to believe God despite what they were experiencing. And because they did, their heart's desire came to pass.

Every vision and every destiny has its appointed time. If you stay faithful to God, He will be faithful to you. God is a faithful God!

4. Alignment for Assignment

When an athlete is preparing for a race, one of the main things he must do is get his body in proper alignment. How well he does during the race will determine how well his body is properly aligned or conditioned.

Being properly aligned is a success matrix. It allows you to glean and be strengthened from those you are associated with. On the other hand, however, if your life is out of alignment, then your road to success will be a lot choppier.

When your car is in need of being aligned, you feel every bump it encounters. But with just some minor adjustments, then it is amazing what it is able to absorb. It is the same with your life, when you take the time to make the minor adjustments in your life for the best, then your life will go a whole lot smoother. I don't know about you, but I like doing things the easy way. Therefore, to get the outcome we want in life, then we must be properly aligned for our assignment.

Dr. Shirley K. Clark

Chapter 3

Elijah's Pattern

Dr. Shirley K. Clark

Elijah, the prophet, is one of the prophets in the Bible that I consider to be a *birthing* prophet. He was one that knew how to birth the will and purpose of God into existence. When Elijah recognized that God wanted to birth destiny through him, he would get in a birthing position.

During the reign of King Ahab judgment was upon the land. The heavens were shut up for three and a half years and there was no rain. Drought encompassed the land. So when it was time for rain to come upon the earth again, God commissioned Elijah to go and release the rain.

It says in I Kings 18:42, **"And Elijah went up to the top of Carmel, and he cast himself down upon the earth, and put his face between his knees."** In this verse there were four things that Elijah did that facilitated his prayer being answered:

1. Found a proper location

2. Humbled himself

3. Got in the birthing position

4. Persevered in prayer

I believe this is a pattern the body of Christ should emulate when desiring change within their lives.

Found a proper location: Elijah went to the top of Mount Carmel to pray. Mount Carmel was Elijah's prayer closet. When birthing out dreams and visions, it is imperative that you locate the place where you commune with God on a regular basis. Often when God is doing something in your life, it requires isolation. It requires getting alone with God and closing out all external factors that can easily distract you from focusing on your goal. *"But thou, when thou prayest enter into thy closet, and when thou hast shut thy door, pray to thy Father which is in secret; and thy Father which seeth in secret shall reward thee openly" (Matthew 6:6).*

Our environment must be conducive for intimacy. Setting aside a time alone with God is the right environment.

Humbled himself: Elijah knew if he was going to see change in the situation, he had to humble himself. He didn't want anything to get in the way of God answering his prayer. It says he cast himself down upon the earth. This is a wonderful display of how someone can be so powerful in the things of God, and yet still, so

> *Humility is a trait that is sometimes missing in many leaders' lives today.*

humble. Sometimes we dismiss things in our minds too quickly.

In Elijah's time, he was known as the most powerful prophet in the land. His name was a household name when it came to declaring and decreeing proclamations over things. This is why Elijah was summoned because whatever he declared, it came to pass. But Elijah knew how to humble himself in spite of this. Humility is a trait that is sometimes missing in many leaders' lives today.

2 Chronicles 7:14 admonishes us that if we are going to see change in a situation, we first have to humble ourselves. *"If my people, which are called by my name, shall humble*

themselves"...God was not talking to the sinner man, but He was talking to His people. We must humble ourselves before Him in order to see manifestation of His glory in our circumstances.

Prideful people have always served as hindrances to the Spirit of God moving. Pride will bankrupt our faith. Pride will cause destruction. Pride will demolish a vision. Pride is in direct correlation with sin.

It was pride that caused Satan to be kicked out of heaven. He began to exalt himself above God and because of this, he was cast out.

"How art thou fallen from heaven, O Lucifer, son of the morning! How art thou cut down to the ground, which didst weaken the nations!

For thou hast said in thine heart, I will ascend into heaven, I will exalt my throne above the stars of God: I will sit also upon the mount of the congregation, in the sides of the north:

I will ascend above the heights of the clouds; I will be like the most High.

Isaiah 14:12-14

Got in the birthing position: When Elijah put his head between his knees, it is said that it resembled a woman in a birthing position. He was prepared to do whatever it took for him to see change. Therefore, he positioned himself for change. Likewise, you have to position yourself for change. God cannot birth something through you if you are out of position. So many Christians are in the wrong position when God is ready to bring forth change.

When there is a shift in your life, transition is inevitable. You must be in the place that God requires of you in order for the full manifestation of your dream or vision to come forth in its totality.

Alignment with the seasons and times of God is a must if change is to be released.

> *Perseverance is the gateway for change in the spirit.*

Persevered in prayer: The book of James said Elijah prayed earnestly (intensely, zealously, sincerely) until rain came forth. When you read the remaining verses in I Kings, Chapter 18, it tells how Elijah sent his servant repeatedly to look for rain while he was constantly praying. **"And said to his servant, go up now, look toward**

the sea. And he went up, and looked, and said, there is nothing. And he said, go again seven times. And it came to pass at the seventh time, that he said, Behold, there ariseth a little cloud out of the sea, like a man's hand...and there was a great rain."

Elijah did not get out of his prayer posture until he saw the manifestation of his prayer. He continued in prayer until there was change. Perseverance is the gateway for change in the spirit. When you persevere in prayer, the spirit of importunity is cultivated and/or activated in your life. It is out of this spirit that things will be birthed. If you want the God of Baalperazim (the God of breakthroughs as David declared him to be in the Book of 2 Samuel) to show up; then you have to persevere in prayer.

The Eighth Day Anointing

When I read this text about this encounter years ago, I automatically assumed, since Elijah told his servant to look for rain seven times, that it was the total amount of times his servant went to look for rain. But as I examined the text more carefully, it was actually eight times that his servant went to look for rain.

> *In order for you to reach your destiny, your present must be redefined and realigned to the different times of God for your life through the eighth day anointing.*

I know why I thought this way initially because Elijah told his servant to go seven more times to look for rain and this number stuck out in my mind. Seven is the number for perfection in the Bible and for some reason we look to grab hold to things we can readily identify with, so we can build a doctrine or truth around it. But Elijah actually sent his servant eight times to look for rain -- the initial time; then seven times more. When I looked up the meaning for the number eight, I realized this number carried a greater amount of significance. It was the number that signified a new move of God. It means new order or new creation. It means God is going to release a new order of government in a situation.

It is out of the number eight that new realms and new dimensions in the Spirit are birthed. New wineskin will come forth. New waves and new moves of God will envelope your life. If I had to put a name to it, I would call it "The Eighth Day Anointing." It is the anointing that will propel you into your destiny. It is the dawning of a new day and a release of change. In order for you to reach your destiny, your present must be redefined and realigned to the different times of God for your life through the eighth day anointing.

It was the eighth day anointing that released and ushered in the rain of God upon Elijah's life. The final result: it was a great outpouring and the supernatural power of God was elevated in his life. God wants the same for you. He wants the eighth day anointing resting upon your life, so that new life might come out of you. It is the eighth day anointing that will also give you new insight. It is the eighth day anointing that causes you to adapt and become flexible in the Master's hand.

In the Bible the number eight was used to signify change and a new order in various situations:

- The eighth day was the beginning of a new week
- David was the eighth son of Jesse
- Noah was considered the eighth person in his family
- Josiah was eight years old when he began to reign as king

- After the Feast of Tabernacle, Holy Convocation was on the eighth day

- It was a Roman custom to circumcise on the eighth day

- It was the eighth day that Jesus went to the mountain of transfiguration

- Jesus was dedicated on the eighth day

- Sheaf of first fruit was to be waved before the Lord on the eighth day

It's time to release the rain!

As I close this section, I want to close by prophetically speaking into your destiny. Recording artist, Martha Munizzi says it best, though. God has a plan for your life and the best is yet to come.

YOUR LATTER WILL BE GREATER THAN YOUR PAST!

Birthing Your Destiny

Dr. Shirley K. Clark

www.ingramcontent.com/pod-product-compliance
Lightning Source LLC
Chambersburg PA
CBHW072042290426
44110CB00014B/1553